Prudhoe Castle

Susie West

Introduction

Prudhoe Castle stands high on a natural platform above the River Tyne, almost cloaked by trees, guarding the river crossing and looking north to the Border country. The first castle here was of timber and was one of many Norman castles built along the Tyne from 1070. It was soon strengthened with a stone curtain wall, gatehouse and keep. After the addition of other towers and the final elaboration of the barbican approach in the 14th century, the defences were complete. Fortunately the castle was not destroyed after the English Civil Wars in the 1640s, unlike so many others that were deliberately rendered indefensible. Instead, its medieval defences decayed gradually into the forms seen today.

Prudhoe Castle was the heart of a landed estate, known as the barony of Prudhoe. In the 11th century the king gave this estate to the Umfraville family from Normandy, who held it until the last male heir died in 1381. By a cunning arrangement of purchase and marriage, the estate passed to Henry Percy, first earl of Northumberland. The Percys were by then the most powerful family in the North East, with Alnwick Castle as their dynastic power base. After a period of decline, the second duke of Northumberland reinstated Prudhoe's role as the centre of a working estate, and the present house in the castle was built for his land agent.

The castle's extraordinary continuity of use endured through the 20th century, when the house was divided into flats. Now restored, the castle is still occupied by the present guardians, English Heritage.

Above: Portrait of Hugh Percy, second duke of Northumberland (1742–1817), by Thomas Phillips

Facing page: Prudhoe Castle from the pele yard, looking across the inner ditch to the west curtain wall with the Norman keep beyond

The Tour

An elegant Regency house lies at the centre of Prudhoe Castle. Many medieval structures, however, still stand, including the keep, the chamber block, and defensive walls and towers.

FOLLOWING THE TOUR

The tour begins at the house, and follows a suggested route around the inner and outer baileys before exploring the strategic setting of the great ditches, the enclosed pele yard and the mill. The numbers beside the headings highlight key points on the tour and correspond with the small numbered plans in the margins.

▮ HOUSE

The house was built between 1810 and 1818 for the second duke of Northumberland's land agent, William Laws. It was intended to be a residence for a gentleman and his family, hence the generous number of reception rooms and the good quality of the architectural detailing and finishes. It stands on the foundations of the medieval lodgings range for the castle household and visitors. The south wall of the house has a 15th-century window and a blocked door *in situ*, and the rear wall is also medieval, with blocked fireplaces and windows beneath the plaster.

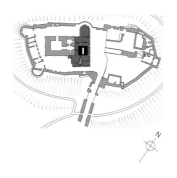

The Newcastle architect David Stephenson (1757–1819) designed the house. Its entrance facade is finely finished in local sandstone, with large and elegantly glazed windows. Their arches are characteristic of early 19th-century interpretations of medieval styles. Architects of this period reworked the defining feature of Gothic architecture, the pointed arch, into a decorative form that had no precedent in medieval buildings. Stephenson was working in this national tradition when he used the Gothic windows to suggest a style appropriate for the setting.

The entrance hall staircase has slender balusters under a mahogany handrail, terminating in a tight scroll, a form typical of the early 19th-century Regency period. The ceiling has a decorative plaster cornice with a tiny arcade of Gothic arches. Pilasters set flush against the wall with linear or reeded decoration define the stair end of the hall. Notice the tiny Egyptian heads with distinctive headdress, set within a frame at the top of the pilasters instead of the more usual capital. While these might seem a surprising detail in an otherwise typically Gothic environment, Egyptian-style references were characteristic of the Regency period.

Above: A small Egyptian head adorning the stair end of the entrance hall – one of the decorative details typical of the Regency period
Left: The elegant entrance hall designed for a gentleman and his family, now restored and furnished in a Regency style

Facing page: Prudhoe Castle from the north-west. The steep drop down to the River Tyne is hidden by the dense tree growth

Collections at Prudhoe

Excavated objects provide a glimpse into the lives of Prudhoe's medieval owners

Archaeological excavations in the outer bailey between 1972 and 1981 have revealed much about life at Prudhoe Castle over centuries of occupation. Some of the excavated objects are now on display in the exhibition. A large quantity of pottery was found, in particular medieval multi-purpose jugs and bowls. The pottery collection spans all phases of the castle's occupation, but is particularly strong for the late 12th and 13th centuries. Although a small proportion of the late medieval pottery was imported from France, the Low Countries, the Rhine and Spain, much of it was made locally.

Personal accessories such as brass buckles, purse frames, bone combs, iron knives and dagger chapes provide a glimpse of the lives of the medieval owners and occupants of Prudhoe. Decorated luxury items including gilded rivets and studs, and fragments of fine Venetian glass goblets, attest to the wealth of the Percys, the richest family in medieval Northumberland; Prudhoe was also owned by a royal duke in the 15th century. The extensive retinue of gentlemen, knights, pages and lesser servants that the family's status required would have filled the castle buildings on their periodic visits. With them came luxurious portable goods, from tableware to tapestries.

Military equipment includes early and later medieval arrowheads, fragments of chain mail and armour, and, with the advent of gunpowder for weaponry in the 14th century, cannonballs. The castle workshops were capable of casting bronze cauldrons, using fired clay moulds, and smithing iron for numerous uses around the castle: horse shoes, nails, rivets and hasps. There are hints of luxury in functional items, such as enamelled pendants from early to mid-14th-century horse harnesses. The excavations also revealed green-glazed roof and floor tiles, and 14th-century bricks from the Low Countries, from the lost medieval buildings.

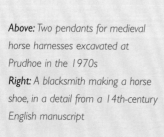

Above: Two pendants for medieval horse harnesses excavated at Prudhoe in the 1970s
Right: A blacksmith making a horse shoe, in a detail from a 14th-century English manuscript

No original furnishings survive, but the interior decoration was probably regularly updated by the comparatively wealthy Laws family. The Regency love of fitted carpets, sumptuous curtains and bright colours carried on through the 19th century, with increasing use of pattern and new chemical dyes for fabrics. The changing uses of the house in the 20th century included subdivision into four small one- or two-room flats after the Second World War, quite a change of status from the luxurious home for one gentry family.

To the right of the entrance hall is the dining room, now the ticket office and shop. Its handsome bow window is typical of Regency architecture. The dining room was usually separated from other reception rooms in larger 19th-century houses to contain any lingering smells of cooked food.

Back across the hall, the first room of the exhibition was a breakfast room in 1856, when the architect Anthony Salvin, who was probably responsible for extending the building at this time, sketched the plan of the house. The second room of the exhibition was used as a sitting room in 1856. There was a further sitting room beyond and a passage out to the kitchen and the back stairs. In the mid-20th century these rooms formed part of two ground-floor flats and were used as a bedroom and living room respectively. On the first floor the light and airy room over the dining room was the 'best parlour', a sitting or reception room with a marble fire surround and a more elaborate plaster cornice. Other rooms on this floor were family bedrooms.

The final room of the exhibition is reached by returning to the hall and turning left. It was originally an outdoor space between the rear wall of the medieval lodgings range and a building of about 1200. The unplastered wall is Norman.

Left: A Regency family parlour, in a watercolour of about 1820. The bow window, plain detailing and comfortable furniture echo the appearance of the Prudhoe house when first built in 1810–18

Below: The iron grate of the fireplace in the former sitting room, with Gothic quatrefoil motifs

Right: The east wall of the Norman first-floor chamber with its fireplace on the left (the flue is visible behind the missing smoke hood). The medieval blocked doorway on the right, noted in a survey of 1586, may have opened on to a gallery connecting with the lodgings range

2 CHAMBER BLOCK

The round arch opens into one of the oldest structures of the castle, the chamber block of about 1200. It was built up against the east wall of the keep, shortly after the keep was completed. It is two storeys high, with the remains of a high-status chamber on the first floor, visible through the modern glass roof of the passage. The front wall was incorporated into the 19th-century rear wall of the stairs still visible at first-floor level. A fireplace, dating to about 1200, now missing its stone smoke hood and supporting pillars, heated the chamber. This feature, and the position of the room next to the first floor of the keep, indicates that it was the private room of the Umfraville lord, the best chamber in the castle.

This chamber block was remodelled about 1330–40 when other alterations were made to the keep. These included the removal of the Norman forebuilding on the north wall, which housed the stairs up to the first-floor keep entrance. New spiral stairs were inserted at the southern end of the chamber block, entered through the square-headed door to the left at ground level. There is a passage from these stairs to the first-floor chamber. As the lodgings range had been built by this time, this passage may have provided a more convenient route from the outer bailey to the lord's accommodation, bypassing the stairs in the forebuilding. To the right, the barrel-vaulted room was probably built centuries after the main structure, when the upper floor was already ruined. Its 19th-century use was as a cold larder.

3 KEEP INTERIOR

The east doorway of the keep opens from the chamber block into the keep basement. This small keep was not intended to be a self-contained dwelling for the Umfraville lord and his family: it was complemented by a Norman great hall and kitchen in the outer bailey. The east doorway was cut through much later, perhaps in the 15th century after the lodgings range had been built, when convenience rather then defence was required. The original door in the north wall appears squat because the floor level was raised over time.

The ground floor of the keep was used for storage, with no access to the upper-floor room, for reasons of defence. Entrance to the first floor was through a north doorway from stairs in a forebuilding. The west wall shows the scar of the gable end of the Norman roof, indicating the great height of this open-roofed upper hall, more private than the great hall in the outer bailey. Within the west wall, best seen from outside the keep, a flight of stairs still ascends to the battlement-level wall walk. With the extensive loss of the east and south walls, no other Norman features remain.

The keep was altered in the 1330s or 1340s to provide better and more spacious accommodation. At this time the Percys were improving Alnwick Castle, and the Umfravilles may have followed their example, perhaps even employing the same masons. Evidence for this activity is apparent inside the keep: the north door was turned into a window, visible as a shouldered arch within the Norman round arch. An extra floor was inserted in the space of the Norman roof, while a shallow-pitched lead roof was added beneath the level of the battlements. Fragments of shouldered-arch windows for this new floor can be seen in the stub of the north wall.

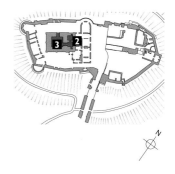

THE KEEP INTERIOR

1 Norman ground-floor entrance, with no access to the first floor

2 Norman first-floor doorway, converted to a window in the 1330s

3 Scar of the gable end of the Norman roof of the keep

4 Well-preserved stairs within the thickness of this wall lead up to the wall walk

5 Pair of 14th-century windows lighting the new floor inserted in the Norman roof space

4 KEEP EXTERIOR AND INNER BAILEY

Leaving the keep through the north doorway and turning to look back at the north wall, it is apparent that buttresses – structural as well as decorative features that articulate the corners and subdivisions of the facades – are lacking here. This is probably because the Norman forebuilding containing the stairs to the first-floor hall in the keep once stood against this wall. At first-floor level there has been extensive refacing, when the windows and the third floor were introduced in the 1330s or 1340s and the forebuilding was removed. While these alterations gave the Umfravilles more convenient and fashionable accommodation, the nature of the changes to the building makes it difficult to identify the different phases of its development. The refacing has obscured the join between the keep and the slightly later chamber block.

The inner bailey was enclosed by the first stone curtain wall of the mid-12th century, but like much of the wall circuit this was rebuilt after subsidence by the 14th century. Subsidence was partly caused by the construction of the stone circuit on the earth rampart that had formed the first defence of the Norman timber castle. The resulting distortion of the curtain wall over the centuries can be best seen when walking round the inner ditch (see pages 16–17).

The north curtain wall has two doorways, probably dating from the 1330s. One with a shouldered arch opens into a small room within the wall. Another gives access to steps up to a latrine. These are both clues for the existence of a structure against the wall, probably a lodgings block, which has otherwise left no trace. To the left, the external stairs up to the wall walk are well-preserved, as is the outline of a demolished two-storey house – it is not known when this was built or who occupied it.

The west curtain wall is filled by the 19th-century stables and a coach house range (not open to the public), which

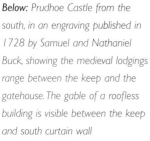

Below: Prudhoe Castle from the south, in an engraving published in 1728 by Samuel and Nathaniel Buck, showing the medieval lodgings range between the keep and the gatehouse. The gable of a roofless building is visible between the keep and south curtain wall

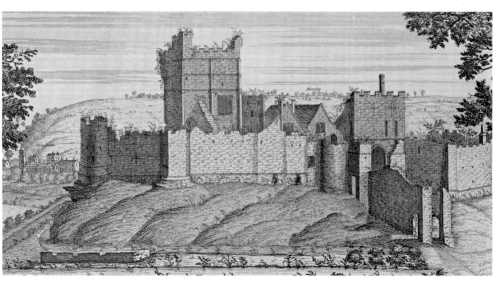

obscure the surviving drum tower in the north-west corner. It is likely that the defences of the castle were upgraded in the 1330s, when the keep was remodelled, as both drum towers and the east tower (see page 13) in the outer bailey are similar to work undertaken at Alnwick Castle at that date. The south drum tower was probably demolished before stables and a granary were built here in the 16th century. This change reflects the decline of the castle's defensive use by this time. The medieval stables for the military garrison would have been located in the spacious pele yard in front of the castle (see page 17).

Moving round to the left, the south curtain wall has an excellent example of an arrowloop and embrasure defending the pele yard area. Nearby, a water trough is set in a recess, possibly from a building identified as 'the Nursery' in a survey made in 1586. Both the west and south walls of the keep have shallow buttresses. The south-east corner of the keep also shows the distinct join with the masonry of the chamber block, which, with its slit windows lighting the spiral stairs, is now embedded within the rear wall of the house.

The rear of the house was extended in the 1850s or 1860s, possibly by Anthony Salvin, who worked for the duke of Northumberland in the 1850s. Salvin's generation reacted against the earlier picturesque Gothic architecture, and developed a scholarly approach to genuine medieval remains. The Stephenson house of 1810–18 had only a ground-floor extension to the rear, reusing medieval walling. The 1850s work created the new back door porch and upper storey, and new windows with simple stone mullions. The south gable roof line was heightened to its present battlemented form.

Reset into the curtain wall side of the carriageway into the outer bailey is a stone carved with two crude heads, much blackened with age. They could be medieval or a 19th-century joke to monitor the comings and goings of visitors.

Above: The arrowloop in the south curtain wall, one of the castle's medieval defensive features
Left: The south-east corner of the keep, on the left, adjoins the taller chamber block and the 1850s rear wall of the house

Above: The castle as it may have looked at the peak of its development in the 15th century, with its massive great hall dominating the outer bailey

5 OUTER BAILEY

The outer bailey was the more public area of the castle, entered directly from the gatehouse and containing the lower-status service buildings as well as the multi-purpose great hall. It was ringed with buildings against the curtain wall. The lodgings range, on the site of the present house, divided the inner and outer baileys and provided high-status accommodation. When the castle was first restored and the house built, by 1818, the outer bailey garden was created, reached by steps up a terrace wall from the house forecourt. The garden was about 1m (3ft) above the medieval level, reflecting the centuries of detritus that had collected here. The decision not to clear the bailey preserved the archaeological evidence, recovered in the 1970s excavations.

To the right of the house, the remains of three great halls have been revealed by excavation. The first great hall was Norman, now hidden beneath the surface. This was replaced in the 15th century by a huge hall 18 × 14m (60 × 46ft), the massive foundations of which are visible. This was built either by the Percys or during the ownership of John, duke of Bedford; in either case, it needed to accommodate the visiting extended household. The increasingly luxurious nature of the hall is shown by the openings made in the defensive curtain wall. Three windows with their stone seats and fragments of

the springing of the arches of the internal openings are still
visible. (The eastern window is the best preserved.) These
windows would have been filled with stone tracery and
stained glass. When the castle's defensive role was greatly
reduced during the 16th century, this large hall was
demolished and a smaller replacement built; it is now seen as
narrower foundations within the floor area of the earlier hall.

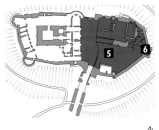

By the north end of the house the curtain wall survives to
its greatest height. The window openings at ground- and
upper-floor levels here suggest that this section was
incorporated into a structure built up against the 15th-
century great hall. Medieval great halls typically had two-
storey blocks built at the dais, or 'high table', end of the hall,
where the lord dined. The parlour on the ground floor of this
block would have been a withdrawing chamber for the lord,
with a bedchamber above. This may have superseded the
Norman chamber block built up against the keep. Directly
in front of the wall, a reset stone sculpted with Neolithic
cup-and-ring marks was used in the medieval building,
showing how building stone was highly valued.

The 'low' end of the great hall is the nearest to the service
rooms and furthest from the lord's table. To the east of this
end of the hall is one room – a buttery and pantry combined,
for storing and serving beer and bread respectively – with
a room above, possibly a high-status withdrawing chamber.
This room, reached by the stairs in the wall, was served by
a latrine, the remains of which lie in the curtain wall.

The kitchen in the north-east corner was built in several
phases, and a plinth and a doorway are visible leading back
towards the service room, once an external wall. To the right,
a brewhouse built against the east tower was referred to in
the 1586 survey. A water trough and the base of the brewing
vat survive, the latter with fire-reddened stones.

6 EAST TOWER

The east tower (not open to the public) was added when
the drum towers were built in the early to mid-14th century.
The original masonry can be seen on the ground floor but
also includes the steps up to the wall walk. The point at which
the steps are decayed and missing, about 1m (3ft) above the
present ground surface, is the level of the 19th-century
garden. The new stone facing is dated by the Gothic window
to about 1810. Perhaps this tower was restored because it
formed part of the view out from the house. A young couple
rented the upper room here in the 1950s, at the same time
that the house was subdivided into flats. The ground-floor
interior has a plain ribbed vault and two openings for
cross-bow loops. The curtain wall to the right passes over
the site of the earliest gatehouse to the Norman timber fort,
uncovered during the 1970s excavations.

*Below: The east tower in the outer
bailey, built in the 14th century and
part of the early 19th-century
restoration of the castle*

The Changing Nature of Building Conservation

Since the early 19th century, the appearance of Prudhoe Castle has changed with different approaches to repair, restoration and conservation of medieval buildings

PRUDHOE CASTLE. 1703.

Prudhoe Castle's appearance today reflects its history of growth, decay and repair. A conscious decision to protect and preserve some ruined parts for their historical interest was made when the restoration works were undertaken in 1808–18. There was a clear division, however, between the defensive features, which were kept, and the domestic buildings (including the great hall), which were demolished. Perhaps the second duke felt that the important part of the castle's history was its military role. His additions to the site were sympathetic in the use of the same stone, but made no attempt at disguise.

Little else was done during the 19th century, and early photographs show that the ruins were allowed to accrue a picturesque level of vegetation. This was cleared away and further repairs were made in 1912. It is likely that the stout iron ties with decorative cross-shaped ends were inserted in the gatehouse at this time. Their highly visible form would probably not be chosen today, but they do fall into the category of 'honest repair', easily distinguished from earlier work.

After the castle came into the guardianship of the Ministry of Works in 1966, the house was returned to its 1818 layout, providing an opportunity for a research excavation under the floor. At the same time the Victorian terraced garden in the outer bailey was cleared to reveal the foundations of earlier structures underneath. The presentation of the medieval wall foundations was in keeping with the prevailing view that sites should be presented with the most significant period clearly defined. Thus the Victorian garden was obliterated in favour of the medieval remains. That decision would be harder to justify today, as conservation philosophy now considers the value of all phases of a site's history. The exhibition reflects this viewpoint, using objects from the excavations, however low status, to help tell the castle's story.

Above: A postcard from about 1910 showing the garden in the outer bailey of the castle
Below: The foundations of the late medieval south lodgings, revealed in the 1970s

⁊ LODGINGS AND LATRINES

Excavations of structures against the south curtain wall have shown that they were timber-framed, and possibly served as workshops. The last building, dating from the 15th century, was used as lodgings, with a latrine on the ground and upper floors that discharges through a chute on the exterior of the curtain wall. The scar cut into the stone of the gatehouse end wall shows that the lodging had a steeply pitched roof – it lies underneath a massive iron tie, inserted probably during the early 20th-century restoration to help stabilise the walls.

8 GATEHOUSE, CHAPEL AND WARDROBE

The gatehouse is the only entrance to the castle. Built by 1150, it was originally two storeys high. The north face looks into the inner bailey, and above the string course are the two 13th-century lancet windows of the chapel for the castle household. The gatehouse was heightened in the mid-14th century, when the original battlements were filled in to create a wardrobe on the third storey. (The term 'wardrobe' originally referred to a room for storage, particularly of furniture and household textiles.) The chimney with a battlemented top dates from the 15th century, when the building was used as a lodging. The timber gates in the passage have been recently repaired and dated by dendrochronology to the 1460s.

The east wall has an unusual oriel (projecting) window, with two lancet windows looking east, as is appropriate for the location of an altar. The lower flight of steps was repositioned after 1818, but the medieval steps were set against the lodgings range, and there is a blocked later medieval doorway between the south wall of the house and the chapel steps and curtain wall.

Inside the chapel, to the right of the 13th-century pointed arch in front of the oriel window, is a damaged niche that may have been a piscina, for washing sacred cups. The loss of the upper floor reveals how the arrowslit openings of the Norman battlements were reused as wall cupboards.

Above: These rather crudely sculpted stone heads on a corbel in the gatehouse passageway are typical of Norman carving
Left: The Norman gatehouse with its 14th-century battlements. The original Norman battlements appear in outline above the level of the two large 14th-century arrowslits

Above: Detail from the reconstruction of the castle in the 15th century, showing the control tower, bridge and barbican in front of the gatehouse

Below: The mill stream, which once turned the water-wheel, still follows its medieval course down the valley

Below right: The ruins of the 18th-century mill, below the mill pond dam and the barbican

9 BARBICAN

The tour of the outer defences begins with the barbican, an open structure designed to funnel attackers through a 'corridor'. The approach to the gatehouse was defended firstly by the ditch, crossed by a timber bridge (where the modern rails are). The masonry between the gatehouse and the bridge represents a low tower later added to control the bridge approach – notice that it is not bonded with the gatehouse. Finally, by 1350, when the towers had been added to the curtain wall, the barbican was built between the bridge and the mill pond area. The steps in the wall on either side led up to wall walks for defenders, and doorways opened into the pele yard and the slope of the outer ditch.

MILL

The east (left) door of the barbican leads to steps on to the path around the inner ditch, below which are the ruins of the 18th-century mill. Although this was the last mill building on this site, there had been a mill here for centuries, owned and controlled by the lord. It was the only one available to the villagers for grinding their flour. The stone dam of the mill pond includes some medieval masonry. The stream flows down into a steep wooded dene, or cut, below.

INNER DITCH

The circuit around the inner ditch, proceeding anti-clockwise, provides good views of the details of the curtain wall exterior as well as an appreciation of the steep drop down to the river. Beyond the east tower, the bulky and much rebuilt north

curtain wall starts, and some window openings from chambers and latrines within the wall appear here. The 15th-century great hall window openings make dramatic breaks in the stonework. Further along the path, even Stephenson's elegant Regency bay of the house seems to loom grimly above, perched high on a bastion.

The 14th-century drum tower, where the wall turns south, has arrowslits at each storey. The square holes supported a wooden fighting platform. The rectangular window openings are later, probably dating from the time when the tower was reused for storage, after the 16th century.

PELE YARD

The stone wall running from the tower across the ditch defines one end of the pele yard, where many daily activities in the garrisoned castle took place. It would have been full of sheds, stables and barns. The pele yard was protected by the outer defensive ditches, and by a gate tower added in 1326. A stone chapel, dedicated to St Mary and founded in the 13th century, was located here. This was probably used by soldiers and servants rather than the lord's family.

The south curtain wall is best appreciated from the pele yard. The south drum tower was reduced to just its base by about 1500, and in the 19th century a conservatory was built here. Square holes visible along the top of the curtain wall held a timber fighting platform. The south end of the house, with its original and reset late medieval windows and its 1850s battlements, is intended to blend harmoniously with the surviving medieval structures.

Below: A postcard of the castle in about 1910, showing the conservatory on the base of the south drum tower and the pele yard divided into allotments

Castle, Town and Church

The landscape around Prudhoe Castle has altered considerably with development from the mid-19th century

The setting of the castle has changed enormously since the arrival of the railway line in the Tyne valley in 1835. Then, the tiny village of Ovingham on the north bank of the river clustered around the church that served the vast medieval parish of Prudhoe, the castle buildings and farm were the main features of the south slope, and Prudhoe village on the crest of the hill was a single north–south street. The main route from the two villages passed the castle mill and the castle gate.

By 1861, Ovingham and the parish church with the castle and Prudhoe town were still in what was essentially their geographical relationship in the Middle Ages, with the old roads and the ferry across the broad but shallow river as the main routes. The number of residents in Prudhoe was growing: 566 people in the 1851 census, housed in 70 homes. Ovingham was half this size, with 330 residents.

A colliery established in the 1860s created industrial employment, expansion of the railway and a rising population. As a result, the medieval parish was split and Prudhoe town gained its own church, St Mary Magdalen, in 1881. The first river bridge here opened in 1883. From then on, the main north–south route came through the miners' village at Low Prudhoe, and the castle was bypassed by a new road in the 1930s. The road scheme was completed after the Second World War when the new road went past the medieval crossroads in the centre of Prudhoe. The focus of development in the town changed to the east–west route along the top of the hill. Post-war industrial development intensified and took over the castle farmland. Housing developments added in each decade filled the farmland between the town and the railway.

Below: A marathon runner is cheered on by Prudhoe residents, as shown on this postcard dating from about 1910

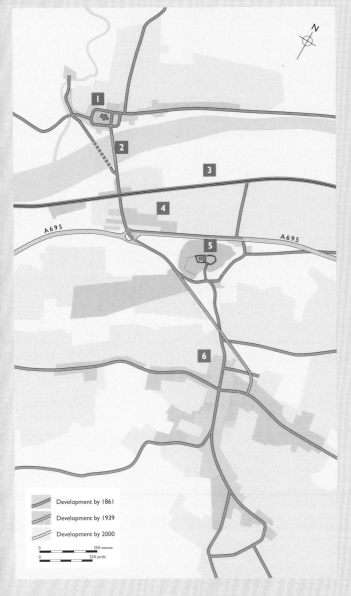

THE DEVELOPMENT OF OVINGHAM AND PRUDHOE

1. Ovingham
2. Bridge
3. Railway line
4. Low Prudhoe
5. Prudhoe Castle
6. Prudhoe town

Development by 1861
Development by 1939
Development by 2000

0   250 metres
0   250 yards

The medieval routes can still be traced on foot. It is possible to follow the medieval lane up from the castle to the centre of old Prudhoe, by turning left after leaving the castle entrance, ascending a steep flight of steps up to the road, crossing this busy new road with care, and picking up the historic Town Trail further up. There is also a medieval bridge crossing a second stream on the path to Orchard Hill fields.

By walking down to the river from the castle, it is possible to follow the medieval route to the ferry crossing. The iron bridge, erected in 1883 after serious flooding of the Tyne, now carries pedestrians, safely segregated from cars, to Ovingham and the ancient church of Prudhoe parish. This church has a Saxon tower, which probably dates to the 10th century, and medieval grave stones are on display in its porch. On the Prudhoe side of the River Tyne, there is also a country park centre and riverside walk to enjoy.

Below: A historic photograph of the tower at the west end of Ovingham church, which probably dates to the 10th century

History

The Umfravilles from Normandy established and developed Prudhoe Castle as the symbolic centre of an estate for nearly three centuries before it passed to the greatest power in the region, the Percy family. The Percys gave the castle a new lease of life with the building of the land agent's house in the early 19th century.

READING THE HISTORY
This section tells the story of Prudhoe Castle from its foundation in the late 11th century to the present day. There are features on the sieges of the castle in 1173 and 1174 (page 23) and the site's more recent history (page 31).

THE NORMAN CONQUEST

The region around Prudhoe was part of the landed estate of
the powerful Saxon earls of Northumberland, and before the
Norman Conquest of 1066 the Scottish kings frequently
invaded the earldom. After the Conquest, the North was
ruled by the earls on behalf of the king, although resistance
and rebellion were so strong that the whole of the northern
English lands were ruthlessly treated in 1080 in a final effort
by the Crown to impose direct rule.

The landscape around Prudhoe was already organised
into estates and small villages by the time of the Norman
Conquest of 1066. The small village on the north bank of the
Tyne at Ovingham had a church with a stone tower probably
dating back to 900 AD. This church lay at the centre of a
parish that straddled the north and south banks of the Tyne.

By 1095 land in northern England was being shared out to
William II's chief supporters. These men owned their land,
known as baronies, by special permission from the king, and
their title of baron reflected this high status. In return, they
guaranteed to supply the king with fully armed knights, or
an equivalent sum of money. There were 21 baronies in
Northumberland: the barony of Prudhoe covered 19 manors
across five parishes.

The first Norman owners of the barony of Prudhoe were
the Umfraville family, who had also been granted the lordship

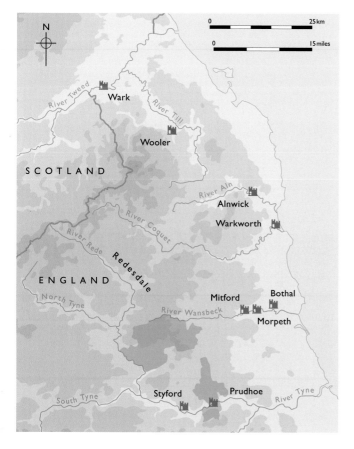

*Above: The castle as it may have
looked in about 1100. It was first
built entirely in timber, but a stone
gatehouse was soon added*
*Left: The nine Norman castles in
Northumberland built with royal
permission by the Norman barons.
The two blocks of land that made
up the barony of Prudhoe are shown
in yellow*

*Facing page: Detail from a late
18th-century watercolour view of
Prudhoe Castle from across the Tyne*

of Redesdale. Robert d'Umfraville was one of the nine barons in Northumberland who were given permission to build a castle in about 1095. Prudhoe Castle, controlling a convenient river crossing, became one of a chain of castles along the Tyne. It is likely that there was no Saxon settlement already established at the castle site, but the village of Prudhoe may already have consisted of a small grouping of farmhouses.

FRACTURED PEACE

Ownership of the border lands between England and Scotland was periodically disputed between the two Crowns. In 1139, the Norman kings granted the titles of earl of Northumberland and of Cumberland to the Scottish kings to keep the peace. As a result, the northern English barons frequented the Scottish royal court, and marriages were made between them and Scottish noble families. Odinel d'Umfraville (d. 1182) had even been brought up in the Scottish court. When Henry II of England reclaimed the earldoms in 1154, he sparked generations of war. Odinel d'Umfraville stayed loyal to Henry, infuriating the Scottish king William the Lion (reigned 1165–1214). William unsuccessfully besieged Prudhoe in 1173 and again in 1174, swearing revenge. Following the second attempted siege, William was captured for ransom in a battle near Alnwick. Odinel was probably sufficiently rewarded to be able to build the stone keep, and was powerful enough to commandeer the serfs of Tynemouth Abbey as a workforce for finishing the castle roofs.

In the 13th century, the Umfraville wealth was increasing. Odinel's son Gilbert married well, to Matilda, the heir to the Scottish earldom of Angus. Their descendants kept the title until the 1350s. When Gilbert d'Umfraville died in 1245, a record was made of his possessions in Prudhoe, which included the villages of Harlow, Ingoe and Kirk Welpington. He owned more than 1000 acres of fields and meadows, which produced an income from rents of £24 a year, while rents from his mills, fisheries and brewhouses raised £45. There was a park for deer around the castle, and 500 acres

Above: The castle as it may have appeared by about 1200 rebuilt in stone, with the keep and aisled great hall

Right: A woman milking a cow, from an early 13th-century English manuscript. When Gilbert d'Umfraville died in 1245, he had extensive holdings of land and control of agricultural industries in and around Prudhoe

The Sieges of Prudhoe

An eyewitness account of the siege of 1173 was written by Jordan Fantosme, clerk to the bishop of Winchester:

The king of Scotland had his pavilions, his tents, and his marquees pitched there, and his earls and barons assembled, and he said to his noblemen: 'My lords, what shall we do? As long as Prudhoe stands we shall never have peace.'

William was forced to give up, but he returned the next year, with an army swelled by French and Flemish soldiers. Luckily, Odinel had been forewarned, and the castle was stocked up with provisions for his men. He slipped out of the castle and rode off to gather support, returning with:

Four hundred knights with shining helms. They will fight with him in the battle, they will relieve Prudhoe with their sharp lances. The siege lasted three days as I know full well.

The besieging army destroyed the castle's farmland and orchards, despoiling crops and gardens, and stripping the bark off the fruit trees. William the Lion still could not take the castle, but worse was to come: as he departed towards Alnwick, Odinel and the knights of Northumberland captured him and killed his Flemish mercenaries:

Now the battle raged fierce and hot on both sides: you could see many javelins hurled and arrows shot, the bold fighting and the cowards fleeing. There was a great slaughter of the unfortunate Flemings, the fields were strewn with their bowels torn from their bodies.

William was taken before Henry II, and imprisoned in Normandy while the terms of Scotland's surrender were worked out. The price for the Scots was heavy – their castles were handed over to English royal control, and William had to pay homage to the English king until Henry's death in 1189.

'My lords, what shall we do? As long as Prudhoe stands we shall never have peace'

Above: A vigorous battle scene in front of a besieged castle, from a 15th-century French manuscript depicting the siege of Troy

Above: The castle was modernised in the 1330s, with the drum towers, the stone lodgings range, the remodelled access to the keep through the chamber block, and the new chapel of St Mary in the pele yard. The defences were completed with the addition of the barbican
Below: Soldiers pillaging a house, in a late 14th-century French manuscript. Prudhoe village suffered raids during the Anglo-Scottish wars

of woodland supplied fuel and building materials. In total, Prudhoe lands produced £110 a year, at a time when the peasantry lived on a few pennies per week.

The medieval village of Prudhoe was a single street, running north–south, on each side of which were laid out the houses of the tenant farmers. There were three great fields made up of individual strips of arable land around the village. The farmers also used meadows to produce hay, and as grazing for their animals, and kept grassland as pasture for their oxen, who pulled the ploughs. Open moorland provided rough grazing for sheep and cattle. The lords of Prudhoe also owned a fishery in the Tyne, where fish traps, a good source of income, were set across the river.

Free tenants were obliged to attend the manor court, held in the castle's great hall. Here the lord heard requests from his tenants, collected rents and fees, and administered local justice. In 1294, Gilbert d'Umfraville II, seventh earl of Angus (c. 1244–1307), asserted his rights to administer punishment in Prudhoe through the gallows, the tumbril (the cart carrying prisoners to execution) and pillory (the wooden frame securing a prisoner by head and hands for public humiliation).

THE NORTHERN MARCHES

Edward I broke 40 years of peace in 1296 by leading his army across the border at the River Tweed, an event that marked the beginning of 300 years of Anglo-Scottish wars. The English Crown defined the counties of Northumberland, Westmorland and Cumberland as the northern marches, and created a distinct legal system designed to cope with hostile action from the Scots (a similar system existed for the Welsh–English border). The marches were subdivided into eastern and western parts, and governed by wardens usually appointed from the ranks of the northern barons, given military and diplomatic duties to defend the border.

Prudhoe Castle continued to guard the Tyne, with a garrison of 40 men-at-arms and 80 armed horsemen. In 1316, Scottish prisoners of war were held in the castle, to be ransomed back to their families. The castle defences were also improved around this time, with the construction of the barbican. The villagers felt the impact of raids by the Scots. In 1303 there were 40 husbandmen (small-scale farmers), who all held 18 acres of land from their lord. This was just enough land to feed their families and to pay the rent. The effect of the Scottish wars was soon felt: in 1325 five of these parcels of land were vacant and new tenants could not be found.

Above: The aisled great hall was replaced by a much larger hall during the 15th century and the timber-framed buildings in the outer bailey were taken down in favour of the stone lodgings block

THE RISE OF THE PERCYS

During the 14th century, the balance of power in the North changed dramatically as the Percy family began to acquire land and castles in Northumberland, extending their influence from Yorkshire. Henry Percy (1368–1406), created first earl of Northumberland by Richard II, struck a deal with the childless Gilbert Umfraville III, ninth earl of Angus (1309/10–1381), for the purchase of half the Umfraville lands when Gilbert died. A more distant Umfraville relative inherited the Redesdale estate, and Percy gained the barony of Prudhoe. Percy also married Gilbert's widow, Matilda Lucy. She was an heiress of considerable wealth, owning the castle and barony of Cockermouth in Cumberland and the castle and manor of Langley in Northumberland. The first earl of Northumberland was now the leading landowner in the North, with Alnwick as the administrative centre of his estates. His desire to maintain his regional power and fear that he was losing influence in national politics would be his ruin.

Below left: Richard II (centre) meeting the first earl of Northumberland (left), depicted in a French manuscript illumination of 1401–5
Bottom: The tomb of Gilbert d'Umfraville, seventh earl of Angus, in Hexham Abbey, in a 19th-century antiquarian engraving

The earl and his son, the famous Harry Hotspur, rebelled against Henry IV in 1403, and Hotspur was killed at the Battle of Shrewsbury. Northumberland rebelled again in 1405, and was a fugitive until his death in battle. The king then gave the

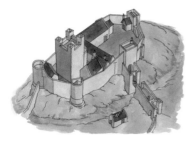

Above: By the time the castle was surveyed in 1586, it was neglected, the great hall had been replaced by a smaller hall and the defunct chapel in the pele yard had been allowed to decay

Below: A Scottish lowland scene showing Falkland Palace in an unenclosed agricultural landscape of the 1630s, similar to the open fields of Prudhoe at this time

barony of Prudhoe to his brother John, duke of Lancaster. He wrote to the king describing the harsh conditions of border life: 'The inhabitants of the marches of both realms daily commit armed incursion, robberies, pillages, prises of prisoners, cattle raids, raids on goods and other acts of war.' During the civil war between the houses of York and Lancaster, known as the Wars of the Roses, Prudhoe Castle was captured by the Yorkist Edward IV in 1464 so that the Lancastrians could not communicate with their temporary allies, the Scots. The Percys finally regained the barony of Prudhoe in 1470.

THE PRUDHOE ESTATE

Although Henry VIII redeveloped royal castles in northern England, Prudhoe does not seem to have been altered during the 16th century. Unlike Berwick, for example, it was far from the threat of coastal attack. Henry Percy, sixth earl of Northumberland (1502–37), was briefly resident during his service as warden of the east march in 1528, and his rebellious brother Sir Thomas Percy returned to Prudhoe Castle after joining the northern uprising known as the Pilgrimage of Grace in 1536. The Catholic seventh earl, another Thomas Percy (c. 1528–1572), also rebelled against Elizabeth I, plotting to put the Catholic Mary, queen of Scots, on the English throne in 1569. The Percys were then forbidden to live in the North but retained ownership of their estates, as the queen wished to avoid replacing them with other nobles who might also prove rebellious.

Subsequently, the Percys had to rely on a system of officials living in their northern properties and collecting rents and fees on their behalf. As part of their estate management, the Percys commissioned frequent surveys of their properties, and these provide insights into the castle's residents and its condition. In 1586, Thomas Bates, a gentleman farmer, leased the castle and 319 acres of mixed farmland for £52 a year.

A survey taken in that year by Thomas Stockdale for the Percy estates listed buildings inside the castle walls including the medieval great hall, kitchen and brewhouse, and commented on their poor state of repair. By 1590, the income raised from Prudhoe was £172. This was not good enough for the ninth earl of Northumberland. He developed a consistent approach to managing his vast estates right through his life. As a result of his insistence that his officials made proper accounts and changed the terms of tenancies, his landed income steadily increased to over £12,000; his lands in Northumberland alone produced £4000 a year. Most of this was achieved by reorganising the layout of village fields so that tenants were more efficient, productive and able to pay higher rents.

There were still open strip fields around Prudhoe in the 1620s, when the bailiff, Mr Orde, recommended that the strips should be amalgamated and redistributed to individual farmers as enclosed fields. The farmers could then rebuild their houses in the middle of the landholdings, instead of returning to the village each evening. This process took a long time to put into action. Over the river at Ovingham only one great common field had survived by 1622, and the Ovingham farmers were pressing for the last remaining open field to be enclosed so that they could afford to pay their rents. Finally, after the death of the ninth earl and the English Civil Wars of the 1640s, the Prudhoe fields were enclosed in the 1650s. The landscape was reorganised into a system of individual farmhouses and fields that still exists today.

Above: Portrait of Henry Percy, ninth earl of Northumberland (1564–1632), from the workshop of Sir Anthony Van Dyck. The earl took a close interest in the management of the Prudhoe estate

Above: The view across the mill pond to the castle, painted at the end of the 18th century by an unknown artist. The top of the tiled roof of the mill, hidden away in the drop beyond the dam and bridge, is just visible

Below: A detail from an illustration of the unrestored outer bailey and gatehouse, published by Sir Walter Scott in The Border Antiquities of England and Scotland *(1814)*

A PEACETIME DECLINE

Following the outbreak of the Civil Wars between Charles I and Parliament in 1642, the royal army controlled the North by 1643. The Parliamentarians allied with the Scottish army, which in 1644 crossed the Tyne. Reaching the ford at Ovingham, they met little resistance at Prudhoe. They marched down to Marston Moor, outside York, and there, in 1644, inflicted a crushing defeat on the northern Royalist army. This marked the final chapter of Northumberland's history as a county of conflict: the Scottish border had been at peace since 1603, when James VI of Scotland inherited the English throne. As a result, Prudhoe Castle finally lost its defensive role.

While the castle was lived in by the earl's officials, such as William Orde, it was kept in reasonable repair. But once the Orde family left in 1672, they were not replaced. The administration of the barony of Prudhoe through the manor court transferred to Alnwick Castle, centre of the Percy estates. Prudhoe Castle was leased to several local farmers, who could afford the high rent but who did not have to keep the castle in repair.

By the 18th century the castle buildings were ruinous. St Mary's Chapel in the pele yard had been reduced to its foundations. The great keep had partially collapsed by the time Sir Walter Scott illustrated Prudhoe in his book about border castles in 1814: he wrote that the outer bailey was 'now so blocked up by the buildings of a farm yard and tenement, that it is not possible to form any idea of its original magnitude'. To many visitors and artists, including J M W Turner, who sketched the castle on a tour of

Northumberland in 1817, Prudhoe Castle was a romantic ruin in a beautiful location.

Hugh Percy, second duke of Northumberland, gave Prudhoe Castle a new lease of life in the early 19th century. He ordered the ruinous buildings to be cleared away and the old medieval residential wing to be rebuilt as the house. Perhaps this was out of pride in his younger son Algernon Percy, who held the title of Baron Prudhoe of Prudhoe Castle from 1816. The duke's architect was David Stephenson, who was born in Newcastle. After training in London he returned to Newcastle in 1783, and All Saints Church there was his competition-winning design.

In 1805, Stephenson was appointed surveyor and architect to the duke of Northumberland, a valuable and constant source of commissions. As well as the monumental column that dominates the southern route into Alnwick town, erected by grateful tenants of the Percys in 1816, he designed farmhouses across the Northumberland estates, and small parts of Alnwick Castle. His responsibility for designing the house at Prudhoe Castle had been forgotten until recently. The rebuilt house was the home of William Laws, land agent to the duke, and his family.

Shortly before the castle was restored, the antiquarian Sir David Smith recorded a simple plan showing the last of the medieval buildings. With the demolition of the ruins of the great hall, kitchen and brewhouse, the now-cleared empty outer bailey was planned as a garden, and a rose garden was planted down in the pele yard, over the site of the chapel of St Mary.

Above: This large-scale plan of the fields, woods and pastures in Prudhoe was made in the 1820s for the estate office. It gives the names of the tenants and owners
Below: The monumental column in Alnwick erected by tenants of the duke of Northumberland and designed by David Stephenson

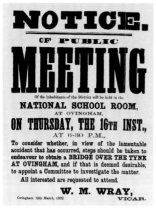

Top: A 19th-century print showing industrial development in this part of the Tyne valley, with Wylam colliery on the north bank of the river, just east of Prudhoe

Above: Poster from 1882 initiating the local campaign for a bridge over the River Tyne between Prudhoe and Ovingham

THE AGE OF STEAM

The revival of the castle was the first of a series of major changes in the parish. In 1835, the railway arrived, following the course of the Tyne out from Newcastle to Hexham. Small-scale mining in the parish had ceased by the end of the 18th century, but the Mickley Coal Company saw potential here and leased mining rights from the duke in 1864 (Mickley is a village east of Prudhoe). The colliery village of Low Prudhoe developed at the foot of the slope up from the station. People still had to use the ford or a ferry to cross the river. After a serious flood in 1882, the iron bridge, funded by public subscription, was opened in December 1883 and is still in use today.

In the 1880s, the castle was advertised for rent, as the Laws family no longer wished to live there. Mr Laws had been advised by his doctor to move to Newcastle; perhaps the exposed winter situation of the castle was too much, even in a comfortable house that had been modernised again in the 1860s. Enthusiasts for Northumberland castles continued to visit, however, sometimes representing official groups such as the Society of Antiquaries of Newcastle, and the Royal Archaeological Institute. There were so many visits that the letting agent commented: 'The privacy of the house is much interfered with by antiquarian visitors – also from the colliery cottagers [who] trespass gathering bramble fruit, bird nesting at rookery & c.'

Perhaps because there were no long-term residents, the castle again decayed, until 1912 when the ruined areas were cleared of overgrowth and repaired, presumably by order of the then duke of Northumberland.

Memories of Prudhoe

'Two massive tortoises roamed about the castle, and the consul let me ride his horse'

Donald McIver recalls his family's connections with Prudhoe Castle before and after the Second World War:

'In the late 1920s, my mother, Elsie, took work as a maid at the castle in order to be near my father, Jack. They married in 1932 and her marriage licence shows her address as Castle, Prudhoe.

'After the War, when friends and I were walking in the castle woods, we met this fellow, José Paniego. I said to him: "My mother used to be a cook here." "Did she?" he said. "Would she like to come back?" So we went round and the place was in a hell of a state – a maid from London couldn't cope with the old stove and boilers.

'Paniego was the Spanish consul in Newcastle. He was a lovely fellow. Mam would leave casseroles and pies in the oven for him. And he'd spoil us rotten. My sister Marion and I had the run of the place. The garden had a lawn and flowerbeds, a fountain, a heated greenhouse and fruit trees. Two massive tortoises roamed about, and the consul let me ride his horse.

'When he left for New York, he couldn't take everything with him. He gave us books from his library and asked dad to sell the wine from his cellar. Sadly, his four-poster bed and the stable stalls were used as firewood by later tenants.

'Dad was asked to be the castle's first custodian in 1969. My wife and I moved with my parents into a flat on the first floor. They were so keen to do the job properly you could hardly get them out of the castle together for the day.

'After dad retired, Mam didn't want to go back. It upset her that they were digging it up. She'd known it when it was a well-kept family house in lovely grounds, and that's the way she wanted it to be.'

Above: José Paniego, the Spanish consul in Newcastle, who lived at Prudhoe Castle
Right: Jack and Elsie McIver on their wedding day in 1932
Far right: Jack McIver, who became first custodian of the castle in 1969

THE CASTLE IN THE TWENTIETH CENTURY

During the 20th century, the landscape around the castle changed dramatically. The farm lands were sold in 1941 to be transformed into the ICI Chemical Works, producing fertiliser. This had an interesting environmental consequence. The waste product was chalk, which was dumped along the riverbank in an area known since the Middle Ages as the Spetchells. Over the years the waste material was colonised by chalk-loving species of plants and insects. After the ICI plant closed in 1963, the site was redeveloped into the present paper mill.

The residential uses of the castle also continued. In the 1930s, a Colonel Nielson rented it. The house was divided up into flats for officers of the Royal Northumberland Fusiliers. During and after the Second World War, the property was used by a consul of the Spanish Embassy. It was then subdivided into four flats rented to local people. The east tower, with just one upper room, was also let in the early 1950s. Conditions were basic, with no running water and only a primus stove and fire by which to cook and keep warm.

In 1966, the Ministry of Works took the site into state guardianship, although it is still owned by the Percys. A series of excavations cleared away compacted debris and masonry, and revealed the original ground level of the inner bailey for the first time in hundreds of years. Rather than being infilled, the foundations of the medieval buildings are displayed as a visible part of the site's 900-year history, and an exhibition about the castle opened in the house in 2005.

Prudhoe Castle.